WITH THE RIVER ON OUR FACE

Camino del Sol
A Latina and Latino Literary Series

With the River on Our Face

EMMY PÉREZ

THE UNIVERSITY OF
ARIZONA PRESS

TUCSON

The University of Arizona Press
www.uapress.arizona.edu

Printed in the United States of America
21   20   19   18   17   16   6   5   4   3   2   1

ISBN-13: 978-0-8165-3344-2 (paper)

Cover design and illustration by Leigh McDonald

"Dear Celan" and "[Magic needed]" reprinted from *New Border Voices: An Anthology*, edited by Brandon D. Shuler, Robert Johnson, and Erika Garza-Johnson, by permission of Texas A&M University Press, copyright © 2014. "Río Grande~Bravo" and part of "Siphoning Sugar" (published as "Brushland, a sorghum field away") first appeared in *PALABRA: A Magazine of Chicano and Latino Literary Art*, 2011. "The History of Silence" reprinted from *The Wind Shifts: New Latino Poetry*, edited by Francisco Aragón, University of Arizona Press, copyright © 2007, and from Emmy Pérez, *Solstice*, 2nd ed., Swan Scythe Press, copyright © 2011. "El Paso~El Valle" reprinted from *Entre Guadalupe y Malinche: Tejanas in Literature and Art*, edited by Inés Hernández-Avila and Norma Cantú, University of Texas Press, copyright © 2016.

Publication of this book is made possible in part by the proceeds of a permanent endowment created with the assistance of a Challenge Grant from the National Endowment for the Humanities, a federal agency.

Library of Congress Cataloging-in-Publication Data
Names: Pérez, Emmy, author.
Title: With the river on our face / Emmy Pérez.
Description: Tucson : The University of Arizona Press, 2016. | Series: Camino del sol series
Identifiers: LCCN 2016004468 | ISBN 9780816533442 (pbk. : alk. paper)
Subjects: LCSH: Mexican-American Border Region—Poetry. | American poetry—21st century.
Classification: LCC PS3616.E7433 A6 2016 | DDC 811/.6—dc23 LC record available at http://lccn.loc.gov/2016004468

♾ This paper meets the requirements of ANSI/NISO Z39.48-1992 (Permanence of Paper).

CONTENTS

WITH THE RIVER ON OUR FACE

And it's you

                    It is you
            I know it's you
    It's you
            And you
                    And you

    Not one
                    You
            You   You in the bee
                    You   in the leaves bitten
    You in the bitten leaves
                            You
                                    You in the holes
            In the bitten leaves
                                    In the absences
    In the leaves
                    You   You in the absences
                    Of the leaves
                            Of the leaving
    You in the absences
            You here

                            ⁓

    You   in the acrylic
                    You in the acrylic
                                    Smell
                    Of carrizo
                                    In the wind
            In the tree trunk
                    You in the red ants   in the dirt dome
                            You, if I look up
                            You, if I look down
            If I sit on the tree trunk
            And feel the earth
                    Rumbling below
            Through the roots
                    Because the wind and river water

                                        Stir the roots
                              To stir below and below
                      Somewhere deep beneath

                Then I know that it is you and you are earth
                      And the earth is nothing more than you

                                        ⁓

          And you are the dragonfly   the dragonfly
                With dotted wings   You
                      Flying   into the leaves
                          The branches   the upright branches
          Upright   You
                Are upright
                      You   in the spaces   between the shadows
          Of the trees on this dirt road   You   in the shadows
                And spaces   in the shadows and snowflake spaces
          In the branch shade   You   in the burnt-sugar
                          Deaths, you

                                        ⁓

                Thirty hawks flying over el río bravo
                              Earth cupping
                                    Water
                              Wind blowing
                      River in the opposite direction
                              Sun lit-up river
                      Sun white-silvers the river

                Is this what it's like
                To feel you   as water
          Carrizo-swaying   water
              Struggling upstream in the sun

                                        Is that you
                                  In the thousand
                                    Silver rivers

                                        ⁓

What I meant to say   is that a long-billed thrasher
            Didn't fly away

                              ⌒

What I meant to say   is that I am not you
            I am not you   not you
                        I don't mean to suggest
                                    That we are the same
                        We're not
            That's why I like you

                              ⌒

            It's vampiric   the way the mosquitos bite
            It's vampiric   the way they find
                        And bite only me it seems
It's vampiric   the way that I am thinking about you

                              ⌒

A braid of berries
            Spat out
With seeds   and chapulines
            Scat out
            Seeds and chapulines

A braid of rat fur
            Shat out
            Shat out in a gray braid

                              ⌒

            Bright blue dragonfly   royal blue dragonfly
Green jay with a blue head   bright dragon
            Green jay   green dragon

And I smelled the pile of bobcat scat   the bobcat scat
            And walked over chalky gray feathers
                        Chalky gray-feathered mouse
            Mouse-like scat   mouse transformed into shit

Feathery feathers and it   leaves a chalk stain
         An outline of a chalk stain
                  And then a turquoise dragonfly   flew
               Right over my head   A bright turquoise
         Dragonfly flew right overhead

                              ⌢

               Red dragonfly   red cardinals
         Green dragonfly   gray cardinals
                    Red damsel   red rubyspot
            Chach-a-laca
               Chach-a-laca

                                   Tree branch in the road
                        Thought it was an indigo
                                   Tree branch in the road
                     Thought it was an indigo

                                   Tree branch in the road
                  I thought it was an indigo
                            Snake

                              ⌢

      Blue-winged dancer   Kiowa dancer
                     Rainpool
            Dragon damsel

                              ⌢

      whole rats shat out
      a whole rat flattened out

      whole rats shat out
      whole rats flattened, flattened
      out   yes. whole, whole rats,
            whole little cotton rats

                              ⌢

what I forgot to say is that violence passed there
            blood spilled there
blood spilled here
                        red dragonfly   red dragonfly
            little hawks   little hawks
                  little jacal
            little mud house   blood spilled there
                              I said violence, violence happened here

                                    ⌒

A pile of seed berries gone straight through
A coyote, javelina, fox, raccoon

I want it expired, expelled, expired-expelled

            I want earth to expire it and extol something new
            You
                        You   You
                  You

                              (blue-spotted comet
                                dancer on water

                        red cardinal
                          zooming low
                              into the blushes

            it looks like an indigo up ahead
                  it looks like an elegant indigo)

"... *el río Grande*
flowing down to the flatlands
of the Magic Valley of South Texas
its mouth emptying into the Gulf."

—

"The soil prepared again and again, impregnated, worked on. A constant changing of forms, *renacimientos de la tierra madre.*"

—GLORIA ANZALDÚA

I.

DOWNRIVER

El Valle

What imperative calls the Altamira
orioles to scrap together nests
that stretch like woven raindrops

from sugar hackberries?
The tip of Tejas is an oriole's
nest that whorls into

México like a galaxy.

Siphoning Sugar

—AFTER INGER CHRISTENSEN

what I want to write exists in the exit and entry routes, in the grapefruits that
plural, won't orange. in the citrus ear canal. in the ombligo.

~

it exists in the one-spotted prepona's longest pink tongue

bark-winged mariposa
from Tamaulipas
siphoning sugar

~

fanning inner wings
with turquoise-brushed V exist

and texas lantana like raspas
also called lantana horrida

~

the hooded oriole exists too, looks like a paleta de mango
in the monte less than a mile from Reynosa

~

el Río Grande exists
inside el Río Bravo
resacas and canales

San Benito water tower
with Freddy Fender's portrait

caracoles and ocelots exist
Mexican bluewings

curanderas, curanderos
and frontera dentists

vermilion flycatchers
and red-faced parrots exist

blue kingfisher
green

and wasp combs
like multibullet
round chambers
I want to call honey

cattle egrets white
treble clefs
flanking cattle exist

and a thousand tinsel triangles rippling
over used car lots

in El Valle's Havana Club
"La vida es

un carnaval"
exists

(and you gifting
es mas bello

vivir cantando
exists)

~

parakeets inching
closer on power lines
exist

it's still winter and feels like April

you aren't here

but the parakeets are grackles
blooming green and yellow
I imagine

kissing you
and telling you exists

A woman like a city

Feeling underexposed like a gift
of blurring into a crowd
of clouds under the sun
sanctuary of a music festival,
drinking Modelo Especial, when
a friendly soul smiles this way.

For years didn't let these smiles exist.

—

            Language can be so sexy.
It turns me on, consonance.

—

Trying to feel my way into Sappho's

I would not think to touch the sky with two arms

Sometimes it sounds ecstatic, sometimes
calm, as in clarity, sobriety, sadness
happiness. Sometimes, you are the sky. Each time
leads to the next:

with what eyes?

But not eyes. Some other breath-gathering, not through sight. Of course
touch but only one arm reaches. Or none. One. One enough. An opportunity
passed? Is it active not to touch this way? Don't want to seemingly possess it,
el cielito lindo.

            Now that it's quiet. Now that the sky is there (or I am here).

—

Will the deaths I carry always need
a ceremony, though *Now I'm alive
inside my death* and the others
must still have hearts and breath.

～

I parked far, far away so I could walk, walk, walk, late, late at night, over
the bridge over this capitol's river, over bat roosts and their saltwater guano,
among no one I know.

～

A woman like a city and you albums of songs

～

and when I woke up in the morning I said, to no one, *it's time to leave* (but
meant to write live).

Gone downriver

—WITH TEXT BY CLARICE LISPECTOR

Yes, downriver
to the beach

party: *The Hour*
of the Star, your under-

linings as if finding them later
rolled up in the sheets, *The Pleasure*

of the Text and me humming
sweet nothingness.

Damned and don't know
it. Consciousness:

I am, I am, I am.
The dope essence

of being, breath of life
God. As pleasurable

and penetrating as love.

El Paso~El Valle

El Paso, Tejas, the physical/spiritual time of transformation. *A present
not embraced by the past. A timeless present, a placeless present,
a transient present.* El Paso, *una herida abierta*, where we meet
others in the dust storm. Eyes sting, reveal all that is unspoken.

Every city is El Paso and every paso, a city where we smile and greet
kind neighbors who raise roosters and water tomato plants
as someone o.d.'s near the canal behind our homes and I never saw
his face because I did not look enough beyond obvious beauty.
Ciudad hermana, across the river, parents carry signs with photos of missing
daughters. El Paso of Native Americans who speak Spanglish.
El Paso of every city in the américas, every city on the globe. El Paso
of when I write and think about you, justicia, and writers unafraid,
where we are not healed, comforted maybe in the roosters crowing
in Ysleta barrio without fail, peach trees growing, and lovely neighbors
I romanticize because they remember ancient family members. El Paso

where refineries flame in the middle of the street and greet us with filthy besos.
El Paso, where land is condemned by name and barrio, then "revitalized,"
as if corporate america is an oxygen machine and residents ghosts
who can move out of the condemnations without dying again, further
into the desert, away from the river and bridges to medicine. El Paso,
where adobe bricks cleaner than marble shipped in. El Paso, where the stench
of our shared sewage permeates summer nights. A place where
newspapers tell it slant or leave it out. Every place on this planet,

where my grandmother, exiled from her father's judgment, birthed ten
children. Ysleta, from where my mother was born to her mexicana mother
and tejano father, who exiled himself from the family created in the adobe
home he built too small but with enough room for his own. El Paso,

where you help me love and forgive. Where I allow myself silence, where
your humility is beautiful and brings pain. All the faces of humility in a city.
Where I learned to love but not enough. Where I learned, at the end, that love
is not fearing, El Paso, *una herida abierta*, como El Valle, como Navajo
country, Santa Ana, L.A., Nueva York, where we have to be stronger to see
if we want to love. El Paso that can never be defined, grapples free,

where love for family is indestructible. Where I learn
what you already seem to know. El Paso

that is not Palestine, El Paso that is not Iraq, Afghanistan. El Paso in Iraq
and Afghanistan. The U.S. in El Paso, in Fort Bliss. El Paso in Iraq
in photographs in Sagrado Corazón, Segundo Barrio, with candles
and candles and candles. El Paso that sometimes forgives
my contradictions because it cannot be defined.

El Paso that is not El Valle and is El Valle. El Valle and all the cities
where papis live. El Valle, *una herida abierta*, palabras de Anzaldúa. El Valle
that is not mine. El Paso that is not mine. I don't want anything to be mine.

Hargill, where the living horse told about the deceased one
in Gloria's poem, where cruel knives gleam in the seeming blindness
of night and neighbors whisper atrocities instead of shouting
them. El Valle of yellow kiskadees and green-blue river, El Valle
where Agent Orange was born in a factory planted in the barrio,
DDT and arsenic still in the soil and blood. El Valle,

where I'm learning how to love, astonished. El Valle of brand new
border walls, concrete, rebar, comfort for those who have never touched
this river water. El Valle where we are witnesses with all the senses,
sometimes the words swallowed in helicopters, hurricanes.

El Valle of green parakeets on 10th Street, bobcats and ghosts of ocelots
in the monte, by Boca Chica~Playa Bagdad, where the river cools blue
herons, children, and fisher women and men as it joins the Gulf.
Spring arrives any time there's a splash of rain with sun, and still
a pronounced flowering in February~March—cacti blooming
fuchsia flowers near salt water—and texas tortoise so fucking ancient
at Laguna Atascosa walking in wind, as we walk in wind, in spring
thinking about desire, Celia Cruz, and female and male cardinals in winter.
El Valle where my toronjas are organic and the big red ants consume
every last peach-white bit of pulp when stray beautiful ones fall to dirt
already with a suckhole for the birds. El Valle where each toronja
in my backyard is a miracle of life. El Valle where I'm teachable.
Teachable by people like you who live their lives in order to love.
Because this is why many of us live our lives, but we don't
stop working to notice.

Pero yo ya no soy yo,
ni mi casa es ya mi casa

en El Paso, en El Valle, everywhere.

Downriver Río Grande Ghazelion

Drive into the Valley, past a field of old farm equipment.
Near the tip of Tejas: Sal del Rey, blatant farm equipment.

I never bent into onion fields or declined sweet strawberries.
The kid in everyone's kitchen, escaping farm equipment.

When I think about seeing you, I want to jump on your back.
I confess—you're sexy, luxury—let's paint farm equipment

The color of parakeets congregating, squawking on 10th
Street McAllen power lines, strip mall trees, fading equipment.

99¢ meals. Surreal pickles like vine fetuses in jars.
Wrinkled wienies on a Stripes treadmill, saintly farm equipment.

Julia (te necesito) ¿dónde estás? ¿En el barrio
De nuestra nostalgia? ¿En el Río Grande de Loíza?

                                    let's
                                  weld
                                jade
                              cave
                        excavate equipment
                          repatriate
                                shell and bone
                                  shards and kernels
                                    study hopi
                                      dry farming
                                    dare roman
                                  empire
                              incan terrace farms
                          aztec chinampas
                            mississippi cotton
                                california strawberries
                                  seedless watermelons, grapes
                                    cherries still need their pits
                                      suck and spit them like chew

Sometimes I defer to the blues, tejanas, two chachalacas
Rustling in ébanos, and ébanos in chachalacas

```
                    río
        bravo           ~grande
    caracoles                   snails
        both            spiral
            galaxies
```

Agha Shahid Ali prayed for each couplet's own identity
Sin fronteras. Linked by rhyme, refrain, y su nombre de diosas
                          & colonizers.

Snake, bobcat, great horned owl, pauraque, bats, tlacuache
                          medicine.
Burrowing vato owls protect their land, urban EPT.

Return? To rivers, loves, monte, el chalán? Erase citrus?
So-called fences? Faith in Boca Chica~Gulf of México, fresh salt-
                     water confluences?

             Salt is old, older than cranium.
               What's older? Salt or water?

It's time to move beyond binaries, old loves. Remember eyes.
Not love but eyes—eyes are love. Yes. Remember the smell of skin:

             Go swimming

             El día en que tú naciste / nacieron todas las flores.

The scent of water. *A tolerance for ambiguity*
In nepantla: between Hurricanes Dolly and Alex
             flooding.

```
            Terremoto, huracán
            You lithium
                The grass
                    Mineral, metal
                        Leaf cuts the ants clip and carry
                            Ant path
                                Goat
                                    Sheep crossing
                                        Rio Grande
                                        Gorge
```

It takes hours to defang cactus. You nursed an orange all of
Christmas Day; at night, just before going to bed, you ate it.

A ~ marks your open text unions. Sign your ~name in e-mail,
Feel your flirty ambiguity, friendly besito.

Boca Chica~Playa Bagdad

People on Playa
        None on Boca

Chica beach
Except us

            To touch
            The river mouth

                    Washed up Chocolala
                    Cartons, caguama
                    Bottles, muddy
                    Swirls

            Boca Chica
            Chica's Boca
            Chiquita Boquita
            Boquita es muy chica
            Muy chiple
            Chica, boca
            Boca, chica
            Chica chica chica chica
            Boca boca boca boca
            Bocachica bocachica boca-
            Chica

Use carrizo
Reed to measure
How deep el Río
Sinks before
The confluence

With the Gulf

                    ~
                    ~
                    ~

How deep are we
Before confluence?

~
~
~

Water has no age

~
~
~

When you said you read poetry like Bible verses
I stopped being suspicious of the world

1. Why

Why so much god between us? Maybe because of distance,
as — is distant. Maybe because of invisibility, as god is nowhere
to be seen except in everything. Except in everything.

2. *God loves God*

The poet is a little
   god. You,

     a little god. And
       an adjective,

         when it doesn't give
          life, takes it

         away. The poet is not
      a "little god."

     The poet
   is a rotten

little rhetorician.

The best is (s)*he*
   who prepares

     our daily bread.

      Diosita, diosito, you who
        reads poetry and rivers

         like they will save
       you, not Jesucristo,

    you prepare my daily bread.

Green Light Go

To be a disco ball dangling in a storefront window, in the sun, with a cage on it. To be two and three disco balls, downtown McAllen, spangles of sun and water that grew tangerine skins late February, pink bottlebrush nostrils, buff-bellied hummingbirds. To be mirrors and hexagonal combs, mexican honey wasps, larvae, paper, wax. To make geometry without vocabulary, to be live music—take off your jacket, girl, wear your tank top . . . it's ninety degrees! To be a green light go, downtown Corpus, after cars and trucks zooming on beach sand, before hot tubs. To be an orange sun driving from Anzaldúa's grave, to be a cactus bloom fuchsia, opuntia, Laguna Atascosa, Laguna Madre, to be a watering hole, a mud chimney air vent for crawdad water tunnels. To be a silver lizard run over by tires, a swatch of river on asphalt, to be a bolt loosened from the border wall, to be a peso falling out of the border crossing's revolving slot, to be a coke-bottle dove, a mexican coca-cola, a cooing quorum of lotería cards signing a resolution. To be a goose perched on top of an abandoned sink in a yard, in a town that fords the river, to be the woman stretched on her beloved's grave, returned after decades. To be a kid in juvie, to be her guardian, the judge, the p.o., to be the letters she writes, the words that matter more than food, almost as much as music and more than makeup, nearly suns seen through the mandatory skylight, imagined by the control room monitor. To be el chalán, the last hand-drawn ferry on the river, its ropes pulled by pilots, to be a passenger almost on the other side.

II.

Midriver

The Same Kind of Huecos

Hot and cool springs, navels blend into earths—
there is no exact point in the moving río grande

where we could wade through and snap an imagined
yellow police tape into the dark

bright summer desert
and prompt border patrol

to force reentry from an official
crossing hundreds of miles away

through la Sierra del Carmen back
to the Chisos in Big Bend while Marathon, Texas

sleeps and the near-empty town of Boquillas, México, abandoned
after 9/11, sleeps. No more canoe taxis in waist-deep river allowed

shuttling a few turistas back and forth to spend
an hour and dollars (vending machine change)

on walking sticks, wire scorpions, cerveza,
bean and cabbage tacos. What is in a name,

Río Bravo, Río Grande, when we are the ones certain
that home is north or south or east or west of you, when

Mexican black bears swim-walk across into the Chisos
and froglets the size of sand flies pop up and down on river mud

when our crossing remains a novelty and others lose
wallets and family escaping patrol lights

in the silk of water springs, all the entry and exit routes
and navels where our first scar was once a mother star, and you, río,

are real, in a canyon, not a metaphor,
and not divided as objects are divided.

Left after crossing

River wet
panties
rolled off
the body
in the shade
of an ébano
near a herd
of goats
grazing
on a bluff

or in a monte
home to
bluewings
that
match tree
bark on top
like closed
eyelids

or in a sorghum
field next
to the palapa
where we drink
pitchers of caramel-
colored beer
with a baggie
of ice inside
as a helicopter
and drone
zone overhead

I always hope
she discarded
panties for a dry
pair from a sealed
plastic bag
to enter
Tejas
comfortable

Border Twins, Confluences

Ciudad Juárez~El Paso   *Agua Santa*   Reynosa~Hidalgo

Ysleta~Zaragoza   Los Ebanos~Díaz Ordaz

Nuevo Laredo~Laredo   *Canícula*   Matamoros~Brownsville

Roma~Miguel Alemán   Rio Grande City~Ciudad Camargo

Boquillas~Big Bend   Terlingua Creek

Presidio~Ojinaga   *El diablo en Texas*

Ciudad Acuña~Del Rio   cuates   Eagle Pass~Piedras Negras

Arroyo de las Vacas   Arroyo de los Jaboncillos

Río Conchos   Río Escondido   the Pecos in Texas   Devils

Zorro Creek   Mud Creek   Las Moras   Zacate

Río San Rodrigo   Río Salado   Río Alamo   Río San Juan

Boca Chica   SpaceX   *With His Pistol in His Hand*

Water rising in the San Juan Mountains   Colorado

South Fork   Conejos River   Alamosa

Red River   Rio Pueblo de Taos   turtle dance

Embudo Creek   *In the Gathering of Silence*

Rio Chama   Nambe River   deer dance   Santa Fe River

Galisteo Creek   Jemez River   Bernalillo matachines

the Pecos, NM   *Bless Me, Ultima*

Big River   Great Waters   Female River

Rio Puerco ~ chǝna ~ *Ceremony* ~ Rio San Jose

posoge

paslápaane   mets'ichi chena   hañapakwa

Tó Ba'áadi

The History of Silence

When did it begin?

       Beauty
Intentionally buried.

Don't comment on screaming
It didn't happen—
              Did it happen?

Maybe they didn't think
We'd hear. Of course
They knew we'd fear it.
Silence is memory,
Black space in the mind's violent eye.
Silence is choice.

Don't comment on memory
The screaming
Didn't happen.
Silence

To erase, *erasus*
From to scratch
To scrape
More at rodent to gnaw
Silentium
Absence
Of mention
Oblivion
Oblivisci
To forget
The fact or condition
Of forgetting
Having forgotten
The condition
Or state of
Being forgotten
Or unknown.

Corn is our history.

Why is it called an ear?
An ear hears and after
Eaten the cob remains and remains
And remains.

Sugarcane, shiny reeds
Who would count the inches
Between sections of guitars,
Staff for notes, staff
For tuning circles, frets,
Shadows in between
Or the sweetness contained inside
Telephone wires
Let's talk
Like marionettes
Little leather boots
Against pregnant stomach.
Is the uterus
Pregnant or the
Woman?
Spiritbody within the spirit
Or body.
Can the spirit control anything?

Fret
From *frezzan* to devour
Akin to *ezzan* to eat.
To eat or gnaw into, Corrode, Fray, Rub, Chaff, to cause to suffer
Emotional Strain, Vex. To pass time as in fretting. Agitate, Ripple,
Wear, to become Agitated. Grate.

Hands of the puppeteer
Atop the wood cross handle
And the little hook
To hang it up
After playing extinct
Would hang
Like a good fall.

A row of soldiers
A row of bodies
This is my row
Row: a noisy
Disturbance or quarrel.

Fresh corn rows

With silk tassels
I can be tender too
White and flattened
On a stone.
My sisters' bones.
Where are they?
Stalls in pupils
Between rows
In the desert
Dilating
Bullets
Mother
Corn
Utterance. History
Of indigenous.

The murdered women's pictures
Millions of self-portraits.

The Valley Myth

The myth begins with no more nopales, víboras, and sacred hierbas. The rare eagle not immune, a consumer, the snake defanged, desexed like acres.

The myth begins with hiring local workers to uproot anacahuitas, huizaches, mesquites, and in the new millennium, it uproots hundred-year-old sabal palms and plants concrete footings for steel column walls.

The valley myth speaks English, insecticides, pesticides. It says great-tailed grackles and white-tipped doves prefer asphalt parking lots. Tamaulipan brushland deseeded, planted with citrus, shrubs squat and dangling beautiful orange and salmon-colored sweets. The myth begins with flesh, ribbed juice, the pith clean and sour and smooth as snow in imported christmas songs.

The myth needs el Río Grande~Bravo—which needs el Río Conchos and el Río Salado—its channels, canals, irrigation ditches, inner tubes, and interludes, its rafts cutting straight across currents during patrol shift changes. The myth begins again with imported palm trees, green grass lawns, automatic sprinklers, and strip malls with all-you-can-eat buffets.

The myth morphs with good riddance, gets pregnant, eats the toronja's placenta, asks for valley lemons, and buys confetti eggs, already dyed, and filled with shredded deeds and documents.

III.

Río Grande~Bravo

Río Grande~Bravo

(iii) The following immigration officers who have successfully completed basic immigration law enforcement training are hereby authorized and designated to exercise the power conferred by section 287(a) of the Act to use deadly force should circumstances warrant it . . .

~

~

The ambiguity of life, the ambiguity of moments, the certainty
Of moments, the certainty of laws, the ambiguity of laws el
Río Grande~Bravo has an invisible line down its center
An invisible caesura
On water
Where I want to apply stitches
Like skin healing
Border
Into water
Again

Liquid cannot be stitched
Imagined by some Frankenstein doctor
Threading water

~

~

In the first decade of the new
Millennium, Washington
Cuts us off from our river
So folks who have never visited
And never plan to
Don't think as much about the invisible
Crossers

Where there is yet no steel or concrete
Border, waves from high speed patrol
Boats ripple
Agents shine lines of lights in Reynosa's trees
The line as discovery, the line as law enforcement
The sky and trees not la migra's property, nothing here its property
(that's not true)
As they trespass with light
And we drink cerveza
Under a palapa with Winter Texans listening to country

~

~

I am trying to remember my love
Of the poetic line, of poetic breaks
And the patrol
Van hasn't moved in an hour
On the new "levee" at the Old Hidalgo Pumphouse
World Birding Center where it's now easier
To search across and down into the river, into México
U.S. side a concrete wall "levee" disguised with dirt
Dirt piled up to form a mountain

I saw the wall
Before it was quickly covered in earth
In time for the pumphouse centennial celebration
While temporary hires planted indigenous plants
To attract hummingbirds
And painted the museum
While the mariachis played
And the Tejano band played
The wall quickly covered in earth
For agents to drive and walk on

Reynosa's view of it up:
A sheer eighteen-foot white concrete wall

Pumphouse eyes patrol and cross
The river's invisible middle line:

Water momentarily Bravo then Grande
Then Bravo. Always Río or Rio.

~

~

We can't build poems faster
Than the wall's construction

Can't write anything
To halt the wall's construction

~

~

"The Magic Valley" of Texas
Ads lured more
Northern settlers and land thefts
In the huddle with Texas Rangers. The Magic
Valley of disappearances, men marrying
Into land grants, the soil magic, the day
Laborers, canals appear like a manna of new rivers, the Magic
Valley's deeds up sleeves and mountains so magic
They never rose, even with helium,
Or popped.

The Valley as El Valle—
El Valle Mágico, monte y agua,
Tierra sagrada. *Flatlands* of white herons.
We are here.

~

~

All the ambiguity of love
All the ambiguity of death
All the ambiguity of fear
All the ambiguity of sex
All the ambiguity

~

~

Poetic line
As desire withheld
And explored
Or withdrawn
Or held
In that pose.

Poetic line
Rushing to the mouth.

Poetic line as *station of the cross*—the stations of suffering, the stations of empathy. Jesus suffered as travelers do. A bus station, a border patrol station, a gas station, lanes for vehicles traveling in Tejas and Texas, not a translation and a translation depending on the situation and location, a station before dying, a station before resurrection, a water station, velas to Don Pedrito Jaramillo after the Falfurrias checkpoint station that brags numbers of "drugs and aliens seized."

Upriver
In Ciudad Juárez
All the clarity of El Paso walls
Called fences, all the clarity
Of a young man caught walking across the river
Line, the river drained here in its concrete mold
Tattooed with words, images of justicia

The youth's friends run back to Juárez
Some throw rocks from the distance
All the permission of officers' deeds
To use deadly force should circumstances warrant it

Should circumstances warrant
Detaining a youth running back home
Should circumstances warrant
Thrown rocks
Pulled hair, stay here,
Pulled trigger
To the distance

                        (¿Le dio. . . ? ¡Le dio! ¡Le dio!)

We are not rocks
Agents are not guns
We are not rocks / Agents have guns / use guns
Agents are
Hispanic
White
Black
Asian
Native American
Men
Women

The river's middle
Line not ambiguous
When there's no water in the sandy Río
Grande and a few puddles
En el Río Bravo
Channel controlled
Young men are not rocks
Let them run
Let them keep running
Home
Please,
Let them

All the ambiguity of detained women, all the clarity of detained women, all the ambiguity of detained women, all the clarity of detained women, all the clarity of too many agents too soon, trained and untrained, untrained and trained, agents as walls with hands that sometimes grab. All the coyotes before them that grabbed and grabbed. All the women and children who haven't slept. All the women and children knowing what's been done to them. All the banked-on ambiguity of the women's and children's silences. All the banked-on clarity of silences. All the clarity~ambiguity of deportation. All the ambiguity~clarity of trying to cross again.

There is no invisible, shifting line when an unarmed man's on the San Ysidro asphalt, agents with batons and electric shocks—

all the clarity of his saying
Ayúdenme,
Por favor

Señores

Ayúdenme,
Por favor

⁓

⁓

The invisible line as utterance in one breath *(I have something to tell you before death)*

⁓

⁓

Midriver line as poetic line. Lifelines in hands with and without guns. Hands. Want to kiss the hands of our lover before moving elsewhere. Hands. The beloved. Hands.

⁓

⁓

The line is the beloved. Again and again and again. Your prose is poetry. Your ends of sentences do not trail off; you fight for them, that space for additional meaning, that breath dying and not wanting to end. Your ends of sentences expand my mind, querid@, create openings instead of endings. When can I see you again to kiss you or meet you, in person and on the page?

⁓

~

And then you asked me to play with fire, to play with fire on the beach. What I want to touch and touch and touch. What I want to drink like water. What I want to taste: seaweed, salt, grains of sand bluebottle jellyfish spread upon. Their clear life I want to touch and touch and touch. You.

~

~

Duras, *The Lover*—sadness after sex in the daytime—separation from ecstasy, from the beloved, a kind of death in daylight. We imagine dying's easier while sleeping.

~

~

Tal vez / tuve que olvidar cómo

May be / I had to forget how to write, how to feel, how to love, how to make love. *May be / I had to forget how* to teach, how to read, think, how to swim in the confluence
of river and gulf

~

~

The wall builders waved at us with sorry on their faces.

They are making our people build it, says a student, *to keep our people out.*

No time for elegant lines or teaching of form before pumpkin time.

The river rushes past, and people still possess the need to cross it. (Desire and need are different entities.)

The academy's proofs and theories say
The wall's the abstraction it was meant to be
The concrete abstraction in front of our face
Writing on paper cannot tattoo the border
Wall, tattooing the border wall
Cannot eulogize our before-wall existence
No do-good neighborhood coalition would blast away
Graffiti on the white concrete surface
Our concrete surface already buried in earth

Our side not buried for respect of the dead
It is buried in spite of the dead, and the not-yet

Our side
And your side, their side—
Here, your becomes their
From second person to third

~

~

We cannot tattoo roses
On the wall
Can't tattoo Gloria Anzaldúa's roses
On the wall
Roses grow in the earth of white-winged doves
The doves coo all day with roosters at Valle de la Paz
Cemetery, the panteón in Hargill near La Sal del Rey
La Sal del Rey where deer snort warnings
From the monte, warn visitors
Because the freshwater puddles near the saline lake are shared
And deer prints outnumber all others, wedge prints fill with salt
And when the sun beats down on the washed-up body of a crystallized frog
I remember Prietita having to kill and bury her fawn
Before the game warden arrives and incarcerates her papi

And I remember a gardener tending flowers
Was thrown by a car carelessly backing up fast
In a McAllen strip mall parking lot. The gardener
Forced a dizzy smile, spoke only Spanish when he finally stood up.
He didn't want to call attention to his presence
On this earth,

This strip mall earth. And so the driver zoomed off.

And I remember the parakeets eating bottlebrush seeds in spring
Their anxious huddling in fall on urban electric wires
I remember buying cascarones on a spring corner
After my own accidents
I remember Brownsville's red-faced parrots
The ancient tortoise at Laguna Atascosa
Hundred-year-old sabal palms uprooted for the wall's concrete footing
I remember the confluence of river and Gulf at Boca Chica
And the fisher women, men, and children across
At Playa Bagdad, Matamoros

I remember wanting to plant and water roses
como las palabras de Gloria, como la gente
del valle, como mexicanos in the borderlands

And when I wake up in the morning feeling love
And when I wake up in the morning with love
And when I wake up in the morning and feel love
And when I wake up in the morning already loving
How the body works to help us feel it

IV.

Cara

Laredo Riviera

I could love you all day
in a Laredo swimming
pool, ears under water,
eyes to the sky. Clouds

can't hear German
shepherds barking post-
shift before they're detained
near the river, our view

from the hotel room window,
in that dusky, almost stadium
light. Two cities facing each
other. What is it to love

within viewing distance of night
vision goggles and guns, mud
and the Republic of the Rio Grande
Museum? We're tourists skipping

churches, living off of credit
and elotes, trying to forget
our maquiladora conveniences.
We toast compañeros~compañeras

who slide along live conjunto
and sticky floors. We imagine who lives
with each other, who only for the night.
Euphoria more ancient than any vow.

Earth is earth. And kryptonite,
kryptonite. You and me, me and you.

Exit routes

—AFTER INGER CHRISTENSEN

What I want to write exists in the exit routes
in good-byes and I love you's still waiting
in the throat, in eloquent e-mails
without cracking voice or protests, in a T-shirt
left behind that smells of skin and clouds

⁓

Dreams exist, dreams of others' dreams exist
Twenty-six dogs unleashed, chasing me through the streets

⁓

First hurricanes exist,
alone in a home older than myself
bagging up photographs

Electricity out before it rains
No remaining phone battery exists

Folks transported from detention centers
papeles wet or nonexistent
Feds ordering the mortaring
of the wall
Projectiles flying through windows
Shelters do not allow pets

Infants exist   The elderly

⁓

Sun green July hot the next day exists

Moyotes~zancudos

And later, bats

⁓

Trying to drive north
in a rush
exists

La manguera
like a live wire

gasoline-
soaked clothes

⁓

Swarms of snout butterflies
splatting on windshields exist
a hundred miles south of San Antonio

⁓

Returning with new friends exists
kind people with abrazos

family living and buried
near the river

where la planta
sinvergüenza exists

⁓

First stop: Hargill

La poeta's grave
disturbed exists
sunken in several feet

First thoughts exist—

who did this?

~

What did this

~

Plastic slide
tunnel
where we'd kissed

while the neighborhood slept

~

Walking blocks and blocks without sidewalks
exists

~

Heart-shaped leaves, bitten like tickets exist
Zebra heliconian butterflies gathered on the same sweet vine
Cut sugarcane in bowls and bees flying through
sugar skulls, ribbons and marigolds
Día de los Muertos en Reynosa

Sprinkler dewdrops poised like the clearest & kindest eyes
on the longest
green blades of grass in McAllen exist
when I wake up

November

It could be the jaguarundi's
Blood on my face

Upon Obama's presidential interregnum a year before the opening of Anzalduas International Bridge, not named after Gloria Anzaldúa

Could I return
To a canal, a channel
Of the river, see another
Turtle shell in the same
Spot as last year
And think of Sappho?

Now unafraid to bike
Slim dirt paths
Fringed with thick cacti
Until I discover a canopy
Of trees
Autumn
Warm

See the empty Cielo
Bottles, a pañal
Candy wrappers
And know travelers
With children
Crossed and maybe slept
On these paths
I hesitate to call safe
For fear of what will
Be done to them
The travelers
The paths

What does it mean, Snow
Birders, to visit a sanctuary
Only seeking ornithology
Accidentally spotting miles of steel
Columns and saying *finally*

I too love urban parakeets
Not their anxieties
Kiskadees, great-tailed
Grackles
Nighthawks
Even mockingbirds

A friend once said
All movement is hope

I thought stasis a kind of
Hope for me to wait
Through November
And winter
Wait to see my childhood
Bottlebrush trees'
Red flowering in March
In strip mall parking lots
Still blooming for humming-
Birds like a forthcoming
Text message
From the beloved
Enticing as a marquee

And then concrete walls
Arrived in Granjeno
Backyards, Thanksgiving
Bearing dark red
Bugambilia
The beloved still
Far away

The old administration
Ushered in these new-
Old ways
(me, naïve
to think the new admin
might not follow suit)

The border, my home
(without you)
Is a real place.

[No toronjas]

No toronjas
this drought year.

Creamy flower
blossoms arrive
late, no fruit
like a season missed.

White like the pith
we once tore
with plump sections
from the peel.

You in a city
somewhere digging
car out of frozen
snow. Bed

at nightfall. I withhold
watering toronjas
like I withhold
my tongue, here

where it is sweetbitter-
sweet. I would
water them

with the slush
of your winter

thaw if you
too would only
speak.

The Snarling, Whimpering Dogs

—AFTER *WALTZ WITH BASHIR*

When the memories return, twenty-six dogs wake and chase him through the streets. I didn't shoot the neighborhood dogs like the soldier who was ordered to keep them quiet for good upon approaching a new village at night. I didn't have to kill them como Prieta tuvo que matar y enterrar a la venadita para salvar a su familia. I needed the dogs, still need them, like the soldier needed them, and Prietita su venadita. They are waiting for scraps of meat, scraps of gold, a hand to lick. I keep them in the pen. I will open the gate soon, though they find their own ways out, into the alleys, to take long runs at night, pee in the orphaned paloverdes sprouting near trash cans, fuck, and howl, especially when I leave to visit mi querida familia and hometown thousands of miles away.

When we watched border patrol in Laredo place their dogs in a holding cell beside the river, you watched longer, not turning away. In the morning, we walked the bridge to a Nuevo Laredo fence with many-colored erected crosses a los migrantes desconocidos y conocidos, slipped through an opening, and sat in the sliver of river monte in full view of the panopticon. You'd step closer and disappear further and, near banks with less traffic, swim for a bit on the grande side, especially en los remolinos that blur the end, the mouth.

The closest I'd get, water on my hands and feet, were to ribbon snakes, now locked up safe from our gaze at Sabal Palm Sanctuary, closed for lack of funding while the minting of a federal wall that smells like new money is staked inside. I'd like to compare that snake's tongue with the one-spotted prepona's, but the butterfly is rare to this side of the río and everything here is locked up with steel crosses. My dogs.

[Every person]

Every person, every ant path, every mesquite shell peck is a river

The River on Our Face

With el río grande~bravo
            in our face
This river
            at its mouth
            at its source
With you at its source
            its sources
With you at the snow
            the evergreens
The million earth holes
            of water emerging
            emerald
Snakes, Gloria Anzaldúa's
            grave
With this river
            on our face

Neon green anole
            swells its throat
            pink-white
El río bravo~
            grande on its face
Ocelots hunt
            under six
            foot shrub
            canopies
With the drive
            of the Continental Divide
            with the pull
            of tributaries
            in their limbs
Chicharras
            whining in the shade
            rivers
            in their timbals
Females laying eggs
            in branches

The young border patrol officer
            flashes sirens daily

lifts his gun
with the river
on his face

Upriver, Chihuahua
        desert ancestors'
        adobe bricks stand up
        crumble down
With el río grande~bravo
        on our face

You said you loved
        the river
        on my face
You said headwaters
        the source
        el río grande
        rises from its source
        saw the lines around
        our mouths
        saw adobe-brick lines
        exposed

Monsoon season
        granizo pelting
        the facades

        at its source
        in my mouth
        adobe mud
        bricks in my mouth
        the earth
        holes, the sources
        the snow
        avalanches
        granizo
        Río Conchos de México
        grandmothers'
        Cueva de la Olla
        at our face
        Tarahumara
        Rarámuri
Tidal confluences
        in our face

Some crossed
        with nuns during la

                    revolución
el río bravo~grande
                    on their face
Relatives
          disappear
          die detained
          with tributaries
          of many rivers on their face

In Ciudad Juárez, a mother hoped
          her missing daughter
          married a rich American
          with the river far away

Constant helicopters finding heat
          with the river as the source

To the west, crossers lift the tortilla
          curtain
Walk deserts without water
          on their face

Guanajuato ancestors crossed through Cali
          with mirages
          in their face

While
I shower daily
with el valle
river water on my face
Thank you and kiss you daily

Julia de Burgos
with el Río Grande de Loíza
Puerto Rico in your face

Julia
I can now speak of hurricanes
and being a dog at someone's feet

I remember El Paso's Inca doves
          burrowing owls in the morning
          barn owls in El Valle's cemeteries
          great horned owl and mockingbirds
          Harris hawks and pauraques
vecinos carrying signs

two communities
"¡No al muro!"
"¡Segundo Barrio no se vende!"
          with the river on their face

A daughter and mother want their ashes
          scattered
          at Boca Chica
          the river's mouth
          the end, the start
          another source
          crabs collapsing
          into bullets bursting out of holes
          carrizo, bugambilia
          seeds   petals   paper
          rose
          raspas
          the mouth
          the eddies
          the tributaries
          the flow
          Río Conchos de México
          the snow
          granizo
          the pelts
          the sources
          rising

The confluence
of people and god
          tortugas
          ribbon snakes in Roma
          pigs and piglets jumping
          from banks
with the river on their face
          You can hear roosters
               crowing across
                    the water in Miguel Alemán

Hurricanes
          disturb unsettled graves
with the river in our face

You said you don't want archaic chains
          lowering you loudly with obvious labor six feet in
You want to hear the cool chachalacas

with the river on their legs
    flapping
        from ébano to ébano
el chalán
the ropes
the pull
over green
water
under
blue sky
to Díaz Ordaz

I want to hear parrots
    sabal palms
    try again
With the river on our face
    I want no medicine
    no ambition
    with the river in my face
I used to love you
    with the river on my face
I still love you
    when the river's on my face
I made a foot-deep grave
    with the river on my face
I loved other rivers
    with el río grande~bravo on my face

I want to oxbow lake

    in this place where children still speak and lose
        multiple tongues
    in this place where we still lose and grow
        forked tongues
    this place where white herons hunt and drink in resacas
    this place with el río grande~bravo
        in its pipes
        in its lungs
        in our face

V.

Boca

What the Arizona SB 1070 copycat bills in Texas can't abolish

MASSES

SATURDAY

4:00 p.m. ENGLISH

5:30 p.m. TEX-MEX (JAN-FEB-MAR)

7:00 p.m. SPANISH

SUNDAY

7:30 a.m. SPANISH

9:00–10:30 a.m. ENGLISH

12:30 p.m. TEX-MEX (MARIACHI)

5:30 p.m. TEX-MEX

MONDAY 6:55 a.m.

TUESDAY 6:55 a.m.

WEDNESDAY 6:55 a.m.

THURSDAY 7:00 p.m.

FRIDAY 6:55 a.m.

CONFESSIONS

THURSDAY 6:00 p.m.

SATURDAY 3:00 p.m.

OUR LADY OF GUADALUPE PARISH

Mission, Texas

Wildlife Refuge Poetics

Huizache "the source
of a particular honey."

Bees and butterflies
sucking zexmenia.

Mexican trixis
for kids, blue
mistflowers

Texas lantana.
Scarlet-bodied
wasp moths pretending

to be wasps. To be
or not—viceroys
wearing monarchs' outfits.

Giant toads "poisonous
enough to kill
small dogs and cats."

Common green
darners "sometimes
eat hummingbirds."

En El Valle
watch what
you say—the black-

throated magpie jay
smuggled
from Huatulco.

The Montezuma
bald cypress unaware
of the Treaty de Guadalupe

Hidalgo. Gulf
fritillary, roseate
skimmers or spoonbills

shoveling freshwater
invertebrates. Mariposa

cola de golondrina
mariposa de ala azul
mariposas cebras

don't sting. Two-
barred flashers
as caterpillars

feed on poisonous coyotillo.
They don't sting. Neither
do wasp posers. They are

just afraid of dying.

Something awakened and killed off each time a teacher speaks

As I pulled off along the one-car spot
on the Rio Rico bluffs, unwalled
beautiful river, in the mirror
border patrol youth reached for his gun
on the seat of his bronco, his sirens red
rolling bleeps behind me

He walked to my car with two
more agents from other vehicles
—*Didn't you see my lights?*

I kept on to help you pass me
up ahead, I said, pointing where the bluff
widens. The third agent slipped in
front of the first, smiling
as he asked for my driver's license

All three scanned my seats
and floor through windows

Can I now curse the agent's smile,
el jefito de los otros, without cursing him?
Can I curse the anxious one who first reached for that pistol
—holstered seconds later—without cursing him?

I think of the youth I played beats and shared censored
rhymes with in juvie responding to boot camp
officer insults, newly shaved heads, orders
to sweep the floor on hands and knees,
their hands as broom and dustpan—

How could I curse the anxious one's anger—
I could be his tía, their tía

How did you know about this place?
asked the smiling jefito

It's on the world birding map

but I didn't bring tourist Tejas
sporting groove-billed anis & green
kingfishers taped to my bedroom wall

He returned my driver's license,
still smiling

and their tías likely not
like me with time and making
time to sit here with a river
instead of a tía grande in the summer.

Dear Celan

How do you move boulders like organs? With language? Sometimes, these words feel pinned under a boulder, when I don't want to feel them. Yours are a *snow-bed*. *Co-earth*. And you fall and fall. *Your course and mine was the boulder's flight*. For a time, I was moved by Lorca's *verde que te quiero verde* before border patrol youth reached for his gun at the Rio Rico bluffs. There was a time when I spent time with the chicharras and remembered *co-planet*, planets in orbit, everything manic green. When I starve the grass and starve the creatures of grass, even the chiggers, what becomes of me?

[Magic needed]

Magic needed. A letter to Lorca. Outer space martians to help me translate. A letter I write and sign by Lorca to introduce my poems. Love poems to the beloved. Lorca or Gloria or Jack Spicer needed in the absence of a beloved. Someone who understands María Sabina's wisdom. A chachalaca as a pet. A glass of water for the dead, to help in their journey crossing. The dead and the not-yet. Sometimes I think I only have water to offer. Dark ruby tunas needed, easy to cut from the tops of cactus paddles. Life offers its appendages. Trim the drooping tree limbs before hurricane season, before we mourn their violent losses. But white-winged doves have their nests in the branches. Nighthawks visit. Bats. Bats keep flitting through the neighborhood. Once, I was attacked by a snake and a bat, my beloved totems. Real visceral pain in my thigh and neck woke me up like seeing the agent reach for his gun. It's still there in his hand, in his holster, keeps rising like the walls that put me to a deep sleep, a sleep that needs *The Collected Poems of Langston Hughes* to wake and find Sappho's golden chickpeas growing again along the riverbanks.

I still dream of you

Somewhere between the age
of Jesus & Julia de Burgos,
my fingers smelled sexy
after picking grapefruit.

I think it fair to compare susto
to natural disaster's onslaught. I
was beaded with Atlantic ocean
sweat, clinging to moving branches

like an iguana in a tree just high
enough to avoid kitchen brooms,
small children and dogs, those
who may have loved me most.

And yet El Yunque's lichen spots
bull's-eye the fresh air wounds
of missing the Fajardo Ferry
though I still run towards its wake

as if you are on it like loggerhead
hatchlings to the South Padre shore
without a thought of getting lost
in oceans or someday returning

by some heart to lay eggs
in the borderlands.

[Mitochondrial Tonāntzin]

Mitochondrial Tonāntzin, pray for us now & at the hour
of our parting. Llena eres de tu gracia,

bendita las frutas
de tu boca,

mente
y corazón.

Poesía

Flood resacas that won't go
to the river mouth.
They sit and wait,
breathe dragon~damselflies
the colors of pictograph masks at Hueco Tanks
the colors of windowpanes on the Ysleta adobe casita
the colors of earrings worn for the rainbow dance,
Santa Clara Pueblo's feast day,
colors I've been hoarding away
like thoughts of macaws traded
from rain forests to what is now Chihuahua
desert to what is now called Chaco Canyon
in what is now called New Mexico
miles, not impossible, away,
upriver, up rivers and tributaries.

Ah, I still love you, mockingbird of El Valle
summer, Río Grande
green mosquitos biting
the limbs down.
And chicharras like terrible lawnmowers
on Sunday mornings, evenings
announcing each of my deaths

with the arrival of more
agents and guns.
One new bridge
and concrete wall
near a river town older
than Texas
not unlike Ysleta
though at its edge a convenience store
flies an american and a confederate flag
with harley decals in their centers
like hearts or apples or stars,
mirrors for bikers
riding here from
somewhere not Granjeno.

Ah, mockingbird, I still love you,
remember your summer song,
always a dj's remix
scratching the bark,
the golden-fronted woodpecker's
grip on telephone poles—
even the lonely dog's howl
I swear in there—
the dog named Brownie
I rename Cuauhtémoc—
El Valle sun burning his skin
bringing a fool's gold of kiskadee
as rats walk at dusk
on electric wires
in the alley behind the house
and later tlacuaches emerge
from under the shed
like la llorona's children
to eat grapefruit
in moonlight while workers
play dead in their beds
hoping the sun won't rise
for another hour, six minutes.

No more crying over last year's drought.
No more not
over my lost home
upriver, ancestral
neighborhood.
No more water debt,
Mexican tributaries
filled, flowing for now.
No more hydrilla and hurricane
bacteria choking the flow.

I thought poetry was chiseled
in skin, a ring too tight to remove.

Ah, mockingbird, I wish I could
sound half as close as you.

Staying in the flood

Why the tom
Spraying the screen
Window, why
Floodwater
Left over from
Hurricane Alex
A spring after last summer
Weed seeds sprouting
Downriver

Why the woodpecker's
Off and on wing
Pause causing
Vertigo, why
Confuse herons with
Egrets. Aztlán:
Land of white herons.

Why the sap stains
Like accidents
Why the border patrol
Woman in a blue truck
With camper big
Enough to haul
Livestock. Why
The anacahuita
Flowers, why one
Giant swallowtail butterfly

Why the debris
Of retama flowers
Gathering on asphalt
Edges like
The path of hair
Under your belly button
Or a path of marigold
Petals welcoming
The dead home

And why the busted-
Up nopal like a bullet
Target or a Just-
Married sign
In April
Strung with
Tecate cans
Hitched to an
El Camino—
Why is it still
Blooming
Yellow roses?

Anzalduas Park

Mujer, it's free today, gratis. Four dollars only on the weekends. Signs: No swimming. Watch for snakes. A yellow snake ribbons around live oak roots, river's edge. Kingbird and urraca songs. Police tape still bows the dock a year after Hurricane Alex flood. Across in Reynosa, Anzalduas también, with palapas lining the river, rancheras from a truck, children's laughter I haven't heard in months. Whatever you got on will bring you in—shorts, T-shirts, rolled-up pants. It's 104, and kids with parents and parents with kids, laughing, tossing mud. *¡Pescando tierra!* a girl shouts. I'm on the bank, in plain view of the constable parked behind, watching me from under tree shade. A few men fish from the edge. Jungle gyms and swing sets empty behind us. Border patrol drives through the parking lot. Cops. La migra rides a fast motorboat, moving border water, shifting it the way a drunk dancer pushes sloppy kisses, closer to families wading, playing. Laughter stops. Waves ripple towards both shores.

A man, waist-deep en el río, resumes fishing with a net. A boy catches guppies in a cup.

I wonder how warm the water is today, what it tastes like when some leaks into the mouth. On this bank, two familiar damselfly bluets fuck stuck together. Maybe the song of an ice cream truck will arrive, or a toddler riding a homemade moped. The bluets look like a turquoise and black beaded necklace I would buy.

laguna madre

the tejas tortoise
opens its mouth

and the tongue
of millennia

dry as an ébano pod
survives.

Not one more refugee death

A river killed a man I loved,
And I love that river still

—MARÍA MELÉNDEZ

1.
Thousands of fish killed after Pemex
spill in el Río Salado and everyone
runs out to buy more bottled water.
Here, our river kills more crossers
than the sun, than the singular

heat of Arizona, than the ranchlands
near the Falfurrias checkpoint.
It's hard to imagine an endangered
river with that much water, especially
in summer and with the Falcon Reservoir

in drought, though it only takes inches
to drown. Sometimes, further
west, there's too little river
to paddle in Boquillas Canyon
where there are no steel-column walls

except the limestone canyon's drop
and where a puma might push-wade across,
or in El Paso, where double-fenced muros
sparkle and blind with bullfight ring lights,
the ring the concrete river mold, and above

a Juárez mountain urges
La Biblia es La Verdad—Leela.

2.
Today at the vigil, the native singer
said we are all connected
by water, la sangre de vida.

Today, our vigil signs proclaimed
McAllen is not Murrieta.
#iamborderless. Derechos
Inmigrantes=Derechos
Humanos. Bienvenidos niños.
We stand with refugee children.
We are all human. Bienvenidos
a los Estados Unidos.

And the songs we sang
the copal that burned
and the rose petals spread
en los cuatro puntos were
for the children and women
and men. Songs

for the Guatemalan
boy with an Elvis belt buckle
and Angry Birds jeans with zippers
on back pockets who was found
shirtless in La Joya, one mile
from the river. The worn jeans

that helped identify his body
in the news more times
than a photo of him while alive.
(I never knew why the birds
are angry. My mother said
someone stole their eggs.)

The Tejas sun took a boy
I do not know, a young man
who wanted to reach Chicago,
his brother's number etched in
his belt, his mother's pleas not
to leave in white rosary beads

he carried. The sun in Tejas
stopped a boy the river held.
Detention centers filled, churches
offer showers and fresh clothes.
Water and a covered porch may
have waited at a stranger's house

or in a patrol truck had his body
not collapsed. Half of our bodies
are made of water, and we can't
sponge rivers through skin
and release them again
like rain clouds. Today

at the vigil the native singer
sang we are all connected
by water, la sangre de vida.

NOTES AND WORKS CITED

EPIGRAPHS

". . . *el río Grande* / flowing . . ." and "The soil prepared again and again . . ."
by Gloria Anzaldúa, from *Borderlands/La Frontera: The New Mestiza* (San
Francisco: Aunt Lute Books, 1987).

I. DOWNRIVER

"El Valle": The Rio Grande Valley, South Texas.

"Siphoning Sugar": After Inger Christensen's *Alphabet*, translated by Susanna
Nied (New York: New Directions, 2011).

"A woman like a city": Title after the line "A man like a city" in William Carlos
Williams's *Paterson*, rev. ed (New York: New Directions Books, 1992).

The italicized poem fragments quote Sappho, as translated by Anne Carson,
from *If Not, Winter: Fragments of Sappho* (New York: Knopf, 2002).

"Now I'm alive / inside my death" from "Trading for Heaven" by Li-Young Lee,
in *Behind My Eyes: Poems* (New York: W. W. Norton, 2008).

"Gone downriver": Found text from Clarice Lispector's *The Hour of the Star*, re-
issue ed., translated by Giovanni Pontiero (New York: New Directions Books,
1992). "She embraced herself, longing for sweet nothingness. She was damned
and didn't know it. She clung to a thread of consciousness and mentally repeated
over and over again: I am, I am, I am. . . . She had searched in the deep, black
essence of her own being, for that breath of life granted by God. . . . A sensation
as pleasurable, tender, horrifying, chilling and penetrating as love."

"El Paso~El Valle": "A present not embraced by the past" and "A timeless pres-
ent, a placeless present, a transient present" from Mahmoud Darwish's poem
"The Owl's Night," in *Unfortunately, It Was Paradise: Selected Poems*, translated
by Munir Akash, Carolyn Forché, Sinan Antoon, and Amira El-Zein (Berkeley:
University of California Press, 2003).

"Una herida abierta" from Anzaldúa, *Borderlands/La Frontera*.

"Pero yo ya no soy yo . . ." by Federico García Lorca, from the poem "Romance
Sonámbulo," in *Collected Poems* (New York: Farrar, Straus and Giroux, 2002).

"Downriver Río Grande Ghazalion": "Sin fronteras," "A tolerance for ambiguity," and "It takes hours to defang cactus . . ." from Anzaldúa, *Borderlands/La Frontera*.

El Chalán is the hand-drawn ferry between Los Ebanos, Texas, and Díaz Ordaz, México.

EPT: El Paso, Texas.

"El día en que tú naciste / nacieron todas las flores" from the traditional song "Las Mañanitas."

"You nursed an orange . . ." after "I nursed my orange . . . just before going to bed, I ate it" from Richard Wright's *Black Boy* (New York: Harper Perennial Modern Classics, 2008).

"[Why]": "God loves God" is a line by Jack Spicer from "The Unvert Manifesto," in *My Vocabulary Did This to Me* (Middletown, CT: Wesleyan University Press, 2010).

"The poet is a little god" and "An adjective . . . takes it away" by Vicente Huidobro, in translation by Dave Oliphant. "The poet is a rotten little rhetorician" by Enrique Lihn, in translation by Oliphant. These lines are from "The Poetry and Antipoetry of Chile" by Oliphant, http://www.nicanorparra.uchile.cl/discursos/oliphant2.html.

"The poet is not a 'little god'" and "The best poet is he who prepares our daily bread" by Pablo Neruda (in translation), from "Nobel Lecture: Towards the Splendid City," December 13, 1971, Nobelprize.org, http://www.nobelprize.org/nobel_prizes/literature/laureates/1971/neruda-lecture.html.

"Green Light Go": Thanks to Claude Fields, from whom I borrowed "coke-bottle dove."

II. MIDRIVER

"The Same Kind of Huecos": Since this poem was written, there is now some legal crossing again in Boquillas, with surveillance from the Border Patrol in El Paso.

"Border Twins, Confluences": River names and confluences from Wikipedia entries on the Rio Grande (Río Bravo) and the "List of Tributaries and Subtributaries of the Rio Grande." In this poem, when *Río* has an accent mark, the body of water is in México. The italicized phrases are titles of books by Chicanx and Native authors.

"The History of Silence": Definitions from *Merriam-Webster Dictionary* online.

"The Valley Myth": "Since the 1920's, more than 95% of the original native brushland in [the Lower Rio Grande Valley] has been converted to agricultural or urban use. More than 90% of the riparian habitat on the United States side of the Rio Grande has been cleared." From U.S. Department of the Interior, *Tamaulipan Brushland of the Lower Rio Grande Valley of South Texas*, Biological Report 88.36 (November 1988).

III. RÍO GRANDE~BRAVO

"Río Grande~Bravo": Opening quote from Code of Federal Regulations of the United States of America: Aliens and Nationality, section 287.8, "Standards for Enforcement Activities," (revised 2007).

"Each line should be a station of the cross" by Charles Wright from "Improvisations on Form and Measure," in *Halflife: Improvisations and Interviews, 1977–87* (Ann Arbor: University of Michigan Press, 1989).

The poem references the fatal shooting of fifteen-year-old Sergio Adrián Hernández Güereca in Ciudad Juárez by U.S. Border Patrol agent Jesus Mesa Jr. on June 7, 2010. It also partially quotes a witness astonished by the shooting, as transcribed by the author from video footage of the shooting.

"*Ayúdenme, / Por favor . . .*": What Anastasio Hernández Rojas asked (as captured in a video recording) of more than a dozen Border Patrol officers as they were tasing him in San Ysidro, California, on May 28, 2010. He died shortly after the beating and tasing.

"Tal vez / tuve que olvidar cómo" by Dolores Dorantes and the translation "May be / I had to forget how" by Jen Hofer from *sexoPUROsexoVELOZ* and *Septiembre* (Denver and Chicago: Counterpath Press and Kenning Editions, 2008).

"They are making our people build it to keep our people out.": Graduate student and artist Emi Z. said this when we went to see the wall under construction in Hidalgo, Texas, in early 2009.

Prieta and Prietita are characters in various works by Anzaldúa. Prieta is a character in the prose poem "Cervicide" from *Borderlands/La Frontera*, which is referenced in this poem and in "The Snarling, Whimpering Dogs." I use the two names interchangeably—my use of Prietita emphasizes the young age of the character.

The poem "Río Grande~Bravo" was written simultaneously with the lyric essay "Healing and the Poetic Line," published in *A Broken Thing: Poets on the Line* (Iowa City: University of Iowa Press, 2011). Grateful acknowledgment to the editors Anton Vander Zee and Emily Rosko for inviting me to write an essay on the poetic line, coincidentally the same year I was witnessing the building of the border wall in the Rio Grande Valley. The essay informs the poem and vice versa.

IV. CARA

"November": Jaguarundis are nearly, if not entirely, extinct in the Rio Grande Valley.

"Upon Obama's presidential interregnum a year before the opening of Anzalduas International Bridge, not named after Gloria Anzaldúa": The official name of this new bridge, which opened in December 2009, is spelled without an apostrophe or accent mark. As of 2016, the Texas cities that own the bridge are still hoping it will accommodate commercial traffic interests. In reference to another poem in section IV of the book, **"Anzalduas Park"**: part of the park exists across the river in Reynosa, México, as well. *Anzalduas* may be a plural word.

"[No toronjas]": The word *sweetbitter* is Anne Carson's translation of Sappho. The word is more commonly known as *bittersweet*, but Carson makes the distinction in her new translation from *Eros the Bittersweet: An Essay*, 2nd ed. (Victoria, TX: Dalkey Archive Press, 2006).

"The Snarling, Whimpering Dogs": The line "como Prieta tuvo que matar y enterrar a la venadita para salvar a su familia" means "like Prieta had to kill and bury the little female deer to save her family."

"The River on Our Face": The accent mark on *Río* in *Río Grande* in this poem (and other poems) is meant to encourage the Spanish pronunciation of the word *Grande* as well. The extra syllable of the Spanish *e* is especially important in creating this poem's rhythm and sound.

Gloria Anzaldúa is buried in Hargill, Texas, in the Rio Grande Valley. Her headstone is partially etched with snake imagery, as she explored complex symbol systems for snakes in her work, particularly in the chapter "Entering into the Serpent" in *Borderlands/La Frontera*. Coincidentally, there is often a snake hole or two right near her grave, and I have seen shed snakeskins beside the grave.

La Cueva de la Olla is an archeological site in Chihuahua, México.

"¡Segundo Barrio no se vende!" is a reference to the grassroots activist efforts against eminent domain abuse and urban removal in this historic El Paso barrio in the new millennium.

V. BOCA

"**What the Arizona SB 1070 copycat bills in Texas can't abolish**" is a found poem from a sign outside of Our Lady of Guadalupe Church, Mission, Texas.

"**Wildlife Refuge Poetics**": Most of the poem is comprised of found lines from plant signs at Estero Llano Grande State Park.

"**Dear Celan**": Quotes in italics are from Paul Celan's poem "What Occurred?," in *Poems of Paul Celan: A Bilingual German/English Edition*, rev. ed., translated by Michael Hamburger (New York: Persea Books, 2002).

"**[Magic needed]**" makes a reference to Jack Spicer's poetics: "For Spicer, the poet acts as a receptive host for language, rather than as an agent of self-expression" (Poetry Foundation online, http://www.poetryfoundation.org/bio/jack-spicer). It also references his letter-poems to García Lorca and the humorous work he wrote to himself in the persona of Lorca in the book *After Lorca*, collected in *My Vocabulary Did This to Me*.

The María Sabina reference (in translation): "I like songbirds. Two years ago I bought a chachalaca . . . for eighty pesos. I knew that a storm was coming when the chachalaca began to coo; it was like a companion for me but, Jesus Christ, they robbed it from me. Now I don't have a chachalaca to distract me." From *María Sabina: Her Life and Chants* by Alvaro Estrada, translations by Henry Munn (Santa Barbara, CA: Ross-Erikson, 1981).

Sappho's poem fragment "and gold chickpeas were growing on the banks" is translated by Anne Carson in *If Not, Winter: Fragments of Sappho*.

"**I still dream of you**": "The age of Jesus" by Michelle Otero in *Malinche's Daughter* (South Bend, IN: Momotombo Press, 2006).

"**Not one more refugee death**" takes its title from a vigil held in McAllen, Texas, on July 19, 2014, and makes reference to more than 60,000 unaccompanied minor refugees from Central America who crossed into the United States in 2014, including fifteen-year-old Gilberto Francisco Ramos Juárez, whose body was found on June 15, 2014, near La Joya, Texas.

Epigraph from "Why Can't We All Just Get Along?" by María Meléndez, in *How Long She'll Last in This World* (Tucson, AZ: University of Arizona Press, 2006).

ACKNOWLEDGMENTS

To the Magic Valle of South Texas, magic because of the people and the land, not only the land, as once advertised by those who would come to exploit its riches, river, and people.

With gratitude and respect to my friend Tato Laviera, for your ceremonias indígenas en El Valle and beyond. QEPD.

Sandra Cisneros, Reggie Scott Young, Norma Cantú, the Alfredo Cisneros Del Moral Foundation staff, and its award judges: thank you for the good news call that saved my poetry heart and the funding that made it possible for me to write more poems for this collection. Stephanie Alvarez, Rebecca Aronson, Anel I. Flores, Britt Haraway, ire'ne lara silva, Moisés S. L. Lara, Vicente Lozano, Patricia Machmiller, Maria Miranda Maloney, Pablo Miguel Martínez, Maria Melendez Kelson, Carolina Monsiváis, Michelle Otero, Oody Petty, Kamala Platt, Diana Rico, José Antonio Rodríguez, Orquidea Salinas, Sehba Sarwar, Beatriz Terrazas, Renata Treitel: thank you for the gift of your feedback on this work in its various stages and/or for supporting me in equally significant ways.

Francisco Aragón and Natalia Treviño: thank you for asking questions one San Anto summer that helped me return to my river video footage and better realize my intentions.

With gratitude to the Macondo Writers' Workshop, CantoMundo, the Grind writing community, the Rio Grande Valley and El Paso poetry communities, the Women Writers' Collective of El Paso, the Society for the Study of Gloria Anzaldúa, the crew of El Retorno: El Valle Celebra Nuestra Gloria, the Mexican American Studies program at the University of Texas— Pan American/University of Texas Rio Grande Valley, and many friends not mentioned for fostering a sense of what is possible in "el mundo zurdo."

Muchísimas gracias to Kristen Buckles, Leigh McDonald, Rosemary Brandt, Amanda Krause, Abby Mogollon, and everyone at the University of Arizona Press for your faith in this work and all the work you support and publish.

Thank you to the editors of the following publications for previously publishing several poems in this collection, some in earlier forms: *Acentos Review, Achiote Seeds/Semillas de Achiote, Borderlines Volume Two, BorderSenses, Cuadernos de ALDEEU, Diálogo, Huizache: The magazine of Latino literature, Entre Guadalupe y Malinche, J Journal: New Writing on Justice, The Laurel Review, New Border Voices, Newfound, PALABRA, Paso del Río Grande del Norte, Pilgrimage Magazine, Vandal: a journal of transformative activism through arts.letters.literature.dialogue,* and *The Wind Shifts.*

ABOUT THE AUTHOR

Emmy Pérez is the author of *Solstice*. Originally from Santa Ana, California, she is a graduate of the University of Southern California and Columbia University. A member of the inaugural cohort of CantoMundo fellows, she is also a member of the Macondo Writers' Workshop for socially engaged writers. In 2009, she was the recipient of the Alfredo Cisneros Del Moral Foundation Award. Previously, she was the recipient of the James D. Phelan Award and poetry fellowships from the New York Foundation for the Arts and the Fine Arts Work Center in Provincetown. Over the years, she has facilitated writing workshops in juvenile and adult detention centers in New Mexico and Texas. Currently, she is an associate professor at the University of Texas Rio Grande Valley, where she teaches in the MFA in creative writing and Mexican American Studies programs. She has lived on the Texas-Mexico border, from El Paso to the Rio Grande Valley, since the new millennium.

CPSIA information can be obtained
at www.ICGtesting.com
Printed in the USA
LVHW042102030323
740870LV00004B/318

9 780816 533442